SEP 02 2013

RICHMOND GREEN
905-780-0711

rg

The Wisdom of Pope Francis

The Wisdom of Pope Francis

Edited by David Birch

Skyhorse Publishing • New York

Copyright © 2015 by Skyhorse Publishing, Inc.

All rights reserved. No part of this book may be reproduced in any manner without the express written consent of the publisher, except in the case of brief excerpts in critical reviews or articles. All inquiries should be addressed to Skyhorse Publishing, 307 West 36th Street, 11th Floor, New York, NY 10018.

Skyhorse Publishing books may be purchased in bulk at special discounts for sales promotion, corporate gifts, fund-raising, or educational purposes. Special editions can also be created to specifications. For details, contact the Special Sales Department, Skyhorse Publishing, 307 West 36th Street, 11th Floor, New York, NY 10018 or info@skyhorsepublishing.com.

Skyhorse® and Skyhorse Publishing® are registered trademarks of Skyhorse Publishing, Inc.®, a Delaware corporation.

Visit our website at www.skyhorsepublishing.com.

10 9 8 7 6 5 4 3 2 1

Library of Congress Cataloging-in-Publication Data

Francis, Pope, 1936-
[Works. Selections. English]
The wisdom of Pope Francis / edited by David Birch.
pages cm
Summary: "Collected here are some of the words that have made Pope Francis so beloved that he was even named Time magazine's "Person of the Year" in 2013. Gathered from his speeches, homilies, sermons, and more, the quotations in this book will inspire any reader to become a more thoughtful, humble, and just person. The Wisdom of Pope Francis will appeal to anyone seeking the wisdom of a spiritual leader"-- Provided by publisher.
ISBN 978-1-63220-351-9 (hardback)
1. Francis, Pope, 1936---Quotations. I. Title.
BX1378.7.A25 2015
230'.2--dc23
2014039053

Cover design by Owen Corrigan
Front cover photo (c) AP Images

Ebook ISBN: 978-1-63220-943-6

Printed in China

Contents

Introduction

In March 2013, Jorge Mario Bergoglio became the 266th pope. When he adopted his new name, as has been tradition for popes since the tenth century, he chose Francis in honor of the twelfth-century Saint Francis of Assisi. Pope Francis is the first to have chosen this name (Pope Benedict was the fifteenth pope to have that particular name). This is only one of the ways in which Pope Francis stands out; he is the first pope to hail from South America, he is the first Jesuit pope, and he is certainly the first pope to be chosen Person of the Year by *Time* magazine.

He is also arguably the first pope to have gained such widespread popularity. Pope Francis's willingness to reach out across lines of faith and belief has thrust him into the public spotlight and given him quite a following in the relatively short period of time that he's worn the papal vestments. His quiet but powerful message of humility, mercy, and equality has captured the imaginations of millions, Catholic or otherwise. Throughout his homilies, masses, and speeches, Pope Francis has consistently stressed a belief in and desire for dialogue and the inclusion of everyone.

Pope Francis's unwavering faith in retaining an open Catholic community has garnered him a universal appeal, as has his commitment and devotion to helping the poor and marginalized. Saint Francis dedicated himself to imitating the life of Christ, rejecting all material wealth and living in poverty just as He did. Pope Francis has lived up to his namesake, eschewing the luxury available to the pope for a life of quiet simplicity and joy. He has called on everyone with means to help those without, and he has challenged all of humanity to work toward making the world a more equal, humble, and merciful place.

This book attempts to collect some of the essence of what has made Pope Francis so beloved by all. Although the quotes gathered here are divided into themes, and although they are from different times and speeches, they are all part of one rich and open message to everyone: commit yourself with humility and mercy to the world and to each other as Christ did and you will know peace and joy. It is my hope that those who read through these selected words of Pope Francis will strive to apply his message to their lives. The power that is within all of us to make the world a better and more equal place can sometimes feel hidden. The wisdom and guidance Pope Francis offers can help reveal it.

David Birch

Fall 2014

The Wisdom of Pope Francis

GOOD

*To be saints is not a privilege for the few,
but a vocation for everyone.*

—Twitter @Pontifex, November 21, 2013

We all have a duty to do good. And this commandment for everyone to do good, I think, is a beautiful path towards peace. If we, each doing our own part, if we do good to others, if we meet there, doing good, and we go slowly, gently, little by little, we will make that culture of encounter: we need that so much. We must meet one another doing good.

—Homily, May 22, 2013

Everyone has his own idea of good and evil and must choose to follow the good and fight evil as he conceives them. That would be enough to make the world a better place.

—*La Repubblica* interview, October 1, 2013

•••

What do I do with my life? Do I create unity around me? Or do I cause division by gossip, criticism, or envy?

—*The Church of Mercy,* April 2014

We have at our disposal so much information and so many statistics on poverty and human tribulations. . . . Let us imitate Jesus: He goes to the streets, not planning for the poor or the sick or disabled people that he crosses along the way; but with the first one he encounters, he stops, becoming a presence of care, a sign of the closeness of God who is goodness, providence, and love.

—Address to the National Federation of Misericordie of Italy, June 14, 2014

We need to pass through the clouds of indifference without losing our way; we need to descend into the darkest night without being overcome and disorientated; we need to listen to the dreams, without being seduced; we need to share their disappointments, without becoming despondent; to sympathize with those whose lives are falling apart, without losing our own strength and identity.

—Meeting with the Bishops of Brazil, July 28, 2013

You can, you must try to seek God in every human life. Although the life of a person is a land full of thorns and weeds, there is always a space in which the good seed can grow. You have to trust God.

—*American* interview, September 30, 2013

I am thinking of what St. Ignatius told us. . . . He pointed out two criteria on love. The first: love is expressed more clearly in actions than in words. The second: there is greater love in giving than in receiving.

—From "The Difficult Science of Love" meditation as quoted by *L'Osservatore Romano*, June 12, 2013

We cannot be Christians part-time. If Christ is at the center of our lives, he is present in all that we do.

—Twitter @Pontifex, August 19, 2013

We have observed that, in society and the world in which we live, selfishness has increased more than love for others, and that men of good will must work, each with his own strengths and expertise, to ensure that love for others increases until it is equal and possibly exceeds love for oneself.

—*La Repubblica* interview, October 1, 2013

This struggle [between God and the devil] is a daily reality in Christian life, in our hearts, in our lives, in our families, in our people, in our churches . . . if we do not struggle, we will be defeated.

—Feast of the Archangels,
September 29, 2014

This is important: to get to know people, listen, expand the circle of ideas. The world is crisscrossed by roads that come closer together and move apart, but the important thing is that they lead towards the Good.

—*La Repubblica* interview, October 1, 2013

•••

Christ's Cross embraced with love never leads to sadness, but to joy, to the joy of having been saved and of doing a little of what he did on the day of his death.

—Palm Sunday Homily, March 24, 2013

God did not wait for us to go to Him, but He moved towards us, without calculation, without measures. This is how God is: He is always the first, He moves towards us.

—First General Audience address, March 27, 2013

In your Christian lives, you will find many occasions that will tempt you, like the disciples in today's Gospel, to push away the stranger, the needy, the poor and the brokenhearted. It is these people especially who repeat the cry of the woman of the Gospel: "Lord, help me!" ... We are to be like Christ, who responds to every plea for his help with love, mercy, and compassion.

—Homily at Closing Mass of Sixth Annual Asian Youth Day, August 17, 2014

True joy comes from a profound harmony between persons, something which we all feel in our hearts and which makes us experience the beauty of togetherness, of mutual support along life's journey.

—Homily from Holy Mass for Family Day, October 27, 2013

When Christians forget about hope and tenderness they become a cold Church, that loses sense of direction and is held back by ideologies and worldly attitudes whereas God's simplicity tells you: Go forward, I am a Father who caresses you.

—Christmas interview with *La Stampa,* December 13, 2013

•••

Help one another. That is what Jesus teaches us. This is what I do. And I do it with my heart.

—Homily at Casal del Marmo juvenile detention facility in Rome, March 28, 2013

Care for life! What a beautiful thing one sees—which I know!—that a grandfather, a grandmother, who perhaps can no longer speak, who is paralyzed, and the grandson or the son comes and takes their hand, and in silence cherishes them, nothing more. That is caring for life.

—Homily during mass honoring the Holy Protector of Pregnant Women, August 31, 2005

Rend your hearts to be able to love with the love with which we are beloved, to console with the consolation with which we are consoled and to share what we have received.

—Lenten Letter of 2013, March 14, 2013

MERCY

A bit of mercy makes the world less cold and more just.

—Angelus, March 17, 2013

I think we too are the people who, on the one hand want to listen to Jesus, but on the other hand, at times, like to find a stick to beat others with, to condemn others. And Jesus has this message for us: mercy. I think—and I say it with humility—that this is the Lord's most powerful message: mercy.

—Homily, March 17, 2013

The Lord always forgives us and walks at our side. We have to let him do that.

—Twitter @Pontifex, August 30, 2014

•••

Time and time again he bears us on his shoulders. No one can strip us of the dignity bestowed upon us by this boundless and unfailing love.

—*The Joy of the Gospel*

Today, in concrete terms, an awareness of the dignity of each of our brothers and sisters whose life is sacred and inviolable from conception to natural death must lead us to share with complete freedom the goods which God's providence has placed in our hands, material goods but also intellectual and spiritual ones, and to give back generously and lavishly whatever we may have earlier unjustly refused to others.

—Address to a UN delegation, May 9, 2014

On this Fifth Sunday of Lent, the Gospel presents to us the episode of the adulterous woman, whom Jesus saves from being condemned to death. Jesus' attitude is striking: we do not hear words of scorn, we do not hear words of condemnation, but only words of love, of mercy, which are an invitation to conversion.

—Angelus, March 17, 2013

Jesus wants to love you for what you are, even in your frailty and weakness, so that moved by his love, you may be renewed.

—"The Light of Faith" letter, June 29, 2013

•••

God never tires of forgiving us, but we sometimes tire of asking Him to forgive us.

—First Angelus Address, March 17, 2013

The presence of God among men did not take place in a perfect, idyllic world but rather in this real world. . . .
He chose to live in our history as it is, with all the weight of its limitations and of its tragedies. In doing so, he has demonstrated in an unequalled manner his merciful and truly loving disposition toward the human creature.

—Address at St. Peter's Square, December 18, 2013

Today I would also like to suggest a medicine to you. But someone might think: "The Pope is a pharmacist now?" . . . It is a rosary with which you can also pray the "Mercy chaplet," a spiritual help for our soul and to spread love, forgiveness, and fraternity everywhere. Do not forget to take it because it is good for you, okay? It is good for your heart, your soul, and your whole life!

—Address at St. Peter's Square, November 18, 2013

This is all the Gospel, here; this is Christianity! But this is not sentimentalism or bland "do-goodism"; on the contrary, mercy is the true force that can save man and the world from the "cancer" of sin, from moral and spiritual malaise. Only love can fill the gaps, the negative abysses that evil opens up in our hearts and in history. Only love can do this, and this is the joy of God.

—Angelus Address, September 16, 2013

We must try to facilitate people's faith, rather than control it. Last year in Argentina I condemned the attitude of priests who did not baptize the children of unmarried mothers. This [mindset of the priests] is a sick mentality.

—Christmas interview with *La Stampa*, December 13, 2013

•••

If you go to him with your whole life, even with the many sins, instead of reproaching you, he will rejoice: this is our Father.

—Homily for the Celebration of Penance, March 28, 2014

The joy of God is the joy of forgiveness. It is the joy of the shepherd who finds his lost sheep; the joy of the woman who finds her lost coin; the joy of the father who welcomes home his lost son.

—Angelus Address, September 16, 2013

In his mercy, he never tires of stretching out his hand to lift us up, to encourage us to continue our journey, to come back and tell him of our weakness, so that he can grant us his strength.

—Homily for Marian Day, October 23, 2013

I want to remind priests that the confessional must not be a torture chamber but rather an encounter with the Lord's mercy which spurs us on to do our best. A small step, in the midst of great human limitations, can be more pleasing to God than a life which appears outwardly in order but moves through the day without confronting great difficulties.

—*The Joy of the Gospel*

And the desert within; when we have no love for God or neighbor, when we fail to realize that we are guardians of all that the Creator has given us and continues to give us. God's mercy can make even the driest land become a garden, can restore life to dry bones.

—Easter Sunday Homily, March 31, 2013

Let us become agents of this mercy, channels through which God can water the earth, protect all creation, and make justice and peace flourish.

—Easter Sunday Homily, March 31, 2013

•••

The Church is not the master of the power of the keys, it is not the master, but rather a servant of the ministry of mercy and rejoices every time that it can offer this divine gift.

—Address at St. Peter's Square, November 20, 2013

God does not destroy the serpents, but rather offers an "antidote": by means of the bronze serpent fashioned by Moses, God transmits his healing strength, namely his mercy, which is more potent than the Tempter's poison.

—From the Holy Mass with the Rite of Marriage, September 14, 2014

The image of an open door has always been the symbol of light, friendship, joy, freedom, confidence. How we need to recover these things! The closed door harms us, paralyzes us, separates us.

—Letter on the Year of Faith,
October 1, 2012

It is not easy to entrust oneself to God's mercy, because it is an abyss beyond our comprehension. But we must!

—Homily, March 17, 2013

•••

Only someone who has encountered mercy, who has been caressed by the tenderness of mercy, is happy and comfortable with the Lord.

—Speech at the International Bookfair in Buenos Aires, April 27, 2001

I think we too are the people who, on the one hand want to listen to Jesus, but on the other hand, at times, like to find a stick to beat others with, to condemn others. And Jesus has this message for us: mercy.

—Homily, March 17, 2013

HUMILITY

*If we want to be healed, we must choose the
road of humility.*

*—Address to representatives of the churches and
Ecclesial Communities, March 20, 2013*

We must all think about whether we can become a little poorer. This is something we must all do. How I can become a little poorer to be more like Jesus, who was the poor Teacher.

—To the students of the Jesuit Schools of Italy and Albania, June 7, 2013

Without ignoring, naturally, the specific scientific and professional requirements of every context, I ask you to ensure that humanity is served by wealth and not ruled by it.

—Message to the World Economic Forum, January 17, 2014

You can't govern without loving the people and without humility! And every man, every woman who has to take up the service of government, must ask themselves two questions: "Do I love my people in order to serve them better? Am I humble and do I listen to everybody, to diverse opinions in order to choose the best path?" If you don't ask those questions, your governance will not be good.

—Mass in St. Martha's House, September 16, 2013

To love God and neighbor is not something abstract, but profoundly concrete: it means seeing in every person and face of the Lord to be served, to serve him concretely.

—Address at a homeless shelter, May 21, 2013

•••

Oh, how I would like a Church that is poor and for the poor.

—Comments to journalists, March 16, 2013

If we love God and our brothers and sisters, we walk in the light; but if our heart is closed, if we are dominated by pride, deceit, self-seeking, then darkness falls within us and around us.

—Christmas Eve Mass, December 24, 2013

Often, so often, we find among our faithful, simple old women who perhaps didn't even finish elementary school, but who can speak to us of things better than any theologian, because they have the Spirit of Christ.

—Homily in St. Martha's House, September 2, 2014

The only way to overcome the temptation of corruption, is service. Corruption is pride, arrogance—and service humiliates you. It is humble charity to help others.

—Mass in Santa Marta, June 17, 2014

•••

Only those who serve with love are able to protect!

—Mass for the inauguration of the Pontificate, March 19, 2013

With great wisdom Benedict XVI reminded the Church many times that for man, authority is often synonymous with possession, dominion, success. For God authority is always synonymous with service, humility, love.

—Address to the International Union of Superiors General, May 8, 2013

That is the purpose of our mission: to identify the material and immaterial needs of the people and try to meet them as we can. . . . Love for one's neighbor, that leavening that serves the common good.

—*La Repubblica* interview, October 1 2013

If there is no humility, love remains blocked, it cannot go forward.

—Homily from Mass of the Annunciation, April 8, 2014

•••

Christian humility is not within the virtue of saying: "I am not important" and hiding our pride. No, Christian humility is telling the truth: "I am a sinner."

—Homily at Casa Santa Maria, March 24, 2014

[Saint] Francis abandoned riches and comfort in order to become a poor man among the poor. He understood that true joy and riches do not come from the idols of this world—material things and the possession of them—but are to be found only in following Christ and serving others.

—World Youth Day in Rio de Janeiro, July 24, 2014

An example I often use to illustrate the reality of vanity is this: look at the peacock; it's beautiful if you look at it from the front. But if you look at it from behind, you discover the truth. . . . Whoever gives in to such self-absorbed vanity has huge misery hiding inside them.

—*Vatican Insider* interview,
February 24, 2012

We incarnate the duty of hearing the cry of the poor when we are deeply moved by the suffering of others.

—*The Joy of the Gospel*

•••

Let us ask for the grace of having the wisdom to put ourselves on the margins, for the grace of humility so that we may receive the Lord's Salvation.

—Homily at Casa Santa Maria, March 24, 2014

A person who is not humble cannot hear along with the Church. He hears only what she likes, what he likes.

—Homily, January 30, 2014

•••

The person who is most high among us must be at the service of the others.

—Mass at Casal del Marmo prison for minors, March 29, 2013

Always step outside yourself! And with the love and tenderness of God, with respect and patience, knowing that we put our hands, our feet, our hearts, but then it is God who guides them and makes all our actions fruitful.

—First General Audience address, March 27, 2013

Jesus sends his followers out with no "purse, no bag, no sandals." The spread of the Gospel is not guaranteed either by the number of persons, or by the prestige of the institution, or by the quantity of available resources. What counts is to be permeated by the love of Christ.

—Homily at Mass with Seminarians and Novices, July 7, 2013

The heart of Christ is the heart of a God who, out of love, "emptied" himself. Each one of us . . . who follow Jesus should be ready to empty himself. We are called to this humility: to be "emptied" beings.

—Church of the Gesu, Rome,
January 3, 2014

•••

Humility [makes us understand that] we have been inserted into a community as a great grace.

—Homily, January 30, 2014

All too often we take everything for granted! This happens with God too. It is easy to approach the Lord to ask for something, but to go and thank him: "Well, I don't need to."

—Holy Mass for Marian Day,
October 13, 2013

Today the place for Christ is the street; the place for the Christian is the street.

—Palm Sunday Homily, March 16, 2008

•••

The one who cares for his brother or sister enters into the joy of the Lord; the one who does not do so, however, who by his omissions says, "What does it matter to me?" remains excluded.

—Mass at Military Memorial in Redipuglia, September 13, 2014

It is the task of the wise to recognize errors, to feel pain, to repent, to beg for pardon and to cry.

—Mass at Military Memorial in Redipuglia, September 13, 2014

•••

Only the commandment of love, in all its simplicity—steady, humble, unassuming but firm in conviction and in commitment to others—can save us.

—Te Deum homily, May 25, 2012

POLITICS

Involvement in politics is an obligation for a Christian. We Christians cannot "play the role of Pilate," washing our hands of it; we cannot. We must be involved in politics because politics is one of the highest forms of charity for it seeks the common good.

—To the students of the Jesuit Schools of Italy and Albania, June 7, 2013

To be human means to care for one another! But when harmony is broken, a metamorphosis occurs: the brother who is to be cared for and loved becomes an adversary to fight, to kill. What violence occurs at that moment, how many conflicts, how many wars have marked our history!

—Homily, September 7, 2013

Always protect the common good. This is the vocation of any political figure.

—*Il Messaggero* interview, July 1, 2014

Turning to mutual respect in interreligious relations, especially between Christians and Muslims, we are called to respect the religion of the other, its teachings, its symbols, its values. Particular respect is due to religious leaders and to places of worship. How painful are attacks on one or other of these!

—Message to Muslims around the world, July 10, 2013

But before all else we need to keep alive
in our world the thirst for the absolute,
and to counter the dominance of a one-
dimensional vision of the human person,
a vision which reduces human beings
to what they produce and to what they
consume: this is one of the most insidious
temptations of our time.

—Address to representatives of the
churches, March 20, 2013

Political institutions are secular by definition and operate in independent spheres. All my predecessors have said the same thing, for many years at least, albeit with different accents. I believe that Catholics involved in politics carry the values of their religion within them, but have the mature awareness and expertise to implement them. The Church will never go beyond its task of expressing and disseminating its values, at least as long as I'm here.

—*La Repubblica* interview, October 1 2013

Dear Presidents, our world is a legacy bequeathed to us from past generations, but it is also on loan to us from our children: our children who are weary, worn out by conflicts, and yearning for the dawn of peace, our children who plead with us to tear down the walls of enmity and to set out on the path of dialogue and peace, so that love and friendship will prevail.

—To Israeli president Shimon Peres and Palestinian president Mahmoud Abbas at the Invocation for Peace, June 8, 2014

We are living in a time of many wars and the call for peace must be shouted. Peace sometimes gives the impression of being quiet, but it is never quiet, peace is always proactive.

—*Viva* interview, July 2014

•••

The corrupt man, then, doesn't have friends; he only has accomplices.
—*Il Messaggero* interview, July 1, 2014

Peacemaking calls for courage, much more so than warfare. It calls for the courage to say yes to encounter and no to conflict: yes to dialogue and no to violence; yes to negotiations and no to hostilities; yes to respect for agreements and no to acts of provocation; yes to sincerity and no to duplicity. All of this takes courage, it takes strength and tenacity.

—Invocation for Peace at the Vatican, June 8, 2014

Here, human self-understanding changes with time and so also human consciousness deepens. . . . There are ecclesiastical rules and precepts that were once effective, but now they have lost value or meaning. The view of the Church's teaching as a monolith to defend without nuance or different understandings is wrong.

—*American* interview, September 30, 2013

You cannot be in a position of power and destroy the life of another person.

—*Sobre el Cielo y la Tierra* interview with Rabbi Abraham Skorka, February 1, 2012

•••

If someone is gay and is searching for the Lord and has goodwill, then who am I to judge him? The problem is not having this tendency, no, we must be brothers and sisters to one another.

—Press conference on return flight from World Youth Day in Rio de Janeiro, July 28, 2013

At this point we wonder: is there a way forward in our present situation? Should we resign ourselves to it? Should we allow our hope to be dimmed? Should we flee from reality? Should we "wash our hands of it" and withdraw into ourselves? I not only think that there is a way forward, but also that the very moment in history which we are living urges us to seek and find paths of hope that open our society to new horizons.

—Address from the pastoral visit to Cagliari, September 22, 2013

We are experiencing a moment of crisis;
we see it in the environment, but mostly
we see it in man. The human being is
at stake: here is the urgency of human
ecology! And the danger is serious
because the cause of the problem is not
superficial, but profound: it's not just a
matter of economics, but of ethics and
anthropology.

—St. Peter's Square, June 6, 2013

The book of Genesis tells us that God created man and woman entrusting them with the task of filling the earth and subduing it, which does not mean exploiting it, but nurturing and protecting it, caring for it through their work.

—Appeal against slave labor via Vatican Radio, May 1, 2013

And he says this to everyone, even to non-believers: it is precisely in solidarity unspoken yet practiced that relationships change from considering someone as "human material" or "a number" to seeing him as "a person." There is no future for any country, for any society, for our world, unless we are able to show greater solidarity.

—Address from the pastoral visit to Cagliari, September 22, 2013

How many more sufferings must be inflicted before a political solution to the crisis is found? The work of the Catholic charity agencies is extremely significant: to help the Syrian population, beyond ethnic or religious membership; it is the most direct way to offer a contribution to the pacification and building of a society open to all different components.

—Note by Pontifical Council "Cor Unum" on relief efforts in Syria, June 6, 2013

This dialogue is what creates peace. It is impossible for peace to exist without dialogue. All the wars, all the strife, all the unsolved problems over which we clash are due to a lack of dialogue. When there is a problem, talk: this makes peace.

—Address to students and teachers of Saitama in Tokyo, August 21, 2013

It is necessary to do justice, but true justice is not satisfied by simply punishing criminals. It is essential to go further and do everything possible to reform, improve, and educate the person, so that he matures from every point of view, does not become discouraged, addresses the damage he caused, and can reestablish his life without being crushed under the weight of his hardships.

—Letter to Congress of the International Association of Penal Law, May 30, 2014

Today more than ever, I think it is necessary to educate ourselves in solidarity, to rediscover the value and meaning of this very uncomfortable word, which oftentimes has been left aside, and to make it become a basic attitude in decisions made at the political, economic, and financial levels, in relationships between persons, peoples, and nations.

—Message for World Food Day,
October 16, 2013

Today's crisis, even with its serious implications for people's lives, can also provide us with a fruitful opportunity to rediscover the virtues of prudence, temperance, justice, and strength. These virtues can help us to overcome difficult moments and to recover the fraternal bonds which join us one to another.

—Message for World Day of Peace, January 1, 2014

We are a society that has forgotten the experience of weeping, of "suffering with": the globalization of indifference has taken from us the ability to weep!

—Homily at Lampedusa, August 7, 2013

•••

How many wounds are inflicted upon humanity by evil. Wars, violence, economic conflicts that hit the weakest, greed for money, power, corruption, divisions, crimes against human life, and against creation.

—Palm Sunday Homily, March 24, 2013

May no one use religion as a pretext for actions against human dignity and against the fundamental rights of every man and woman, above all to the right to life and the right of everyone to religious freedom.

—From Papal visit to Albania, as quoted by the *Guardian*, September 21, 2014

War is madness.

—Mass at Military Memorial in Redipuglia,
September 13, 2014

POVERTY & INEQUALITY

Inequality is the root of social ills.
—Twitter @Pontifex, April 28, 2014

The poverty of the world is a scandal. In a world where there is such great wealth, so many resources for giving food to everyone, it is impossible to understand how there could be so many hungry children, so many children without education, so many poor people! Poverty today is a cry.

—To the students of the Jesuit Schools of Italy and Albania, June 7, 2013

Inequality eventually engenders a violence which recourse to arms cannot and never will be able to resolve.

—*The Joy of the Gospel*

Jesus says that one cannot serve two masters, God and wealth. And when we are judged in the Final Judgment, our closeness to poverty counts. Poverty distances us from idolatry; it opens the doors to Providence.

—Interview with Corriere della Sera, March 5, 2014

A way has to be found to enable everyone to benefit from the fruits of the earth, and not simply to close the gap between the affluent and those who must be satisfied with the crumbs falling from the table, but above all to satisfy the demands of justice, fairness, and respect for every human being.

—Address to the Food and Agriculture Organization of the United Nations, June 20, 2013

The measure of the greatness of a society is found in the way it treats those most in need, those who have nothing apart from their poverty.

—Twitter @Pontifex, January 31, 2013

Human rights are not only violated by terrorism, repression, or assassination, but also by unfair economic structures that creates huge inequalities.

—Quoted by the *Guardian*, March 13, 2013

When we are generous in welcoming people and sharing something with them—some food, a place in our homes, our time—not only do we no longer remain poor: we are enriched.

—Address at Varginha, July 25, 2013

We live in the most unequal part of the world, which has grown the most yet reduced misery the least. The unjust distribution of goods persists, creating a situation of social sin that cries out to Heaven and limits the possibilities of a fuller life for so many of our brothers.

—*National Catholic Reporter,* March 3, 2012

[Of early Christian martyrs in Korea]
Their example has much to say to us who
live in societies where, alongside immense
wealth, dire poverty is silently growing;
where the cry of the poor is seldom
heeded and where Christ continues to
call out to us, asking us to love and serve
him by tending to our brothers and sisters
in need.

—Mass for the Beatification of the Korean
Martyrs, August 16, 2014

Among our tasks as witnesses to the love of Christ is that of giving a voice to the cry of the poor, so that they are not abandoned to the laws of an economy that seems at times to treat people as mere consumers.

—Address to the Archbishop of Canterbury, June 14, 2013

God shows the poor "his first mercy."
This divine preference has consequences
for the faith life of all Christians, since
we are called to have "this mind . . . which
was in Jesus Christ."

—*The Joy of the Gospel*

Human beings are themselves considered consumer goods to be used and then discarded. We have created a "throw away" culture which is now spreading.

—*The Joy of the Gospel*

•••

The only thing that I tell you today is look each other in the face, recognize our brother's dignity, and fight so that dignity survives.

—Homily at the Plaza de Constitucion on modern slavery, September 4, 2009

In the case of global political and economic organization, much more needs to be achieved, since an important part of humanity does not share in the benefits of progress and is in fact relegated to the status of second-class citizens.

—Address to a UN delegation, May 9, 2014

There is no worse material poverty, I am keen to stress, than the poverty which prevents people from earning their bread and deprives them of the dignity of work.

—Conference of the Centesimus Annus Pro Pontifice Foundation, May 25, 2013

Let us pray that the Lord gives us the grace to envisage a world in which no one must ever again die of hunger. And asking for this grace, I give you my blessing.

—Campaign Against Global Hunger video message, December 9, 2013

We have created new idols. The worship of the golden calf of old has found a new and heartless image in the cult of money and the dictatorship of an economy which is faceless and lacking any truly humane goal.

—Address to new non-resident ambassadors to the Holy See, May 16, 2013

How can it be that it is not a news item when an elderly homeless person dies of exposure, but it is news when the stock market loses two points?

—*The Joy of the Gospel*

People have to struggle to live and, frequently, to live in an undignified way. One cause of this situation, in my opinion, is in our relationship with money, and our acceptance of its power over ourselves and our society.

—Address to new non-resident ambassadors to the Holy See, May 16, 2013

This is precisely the reason for the dissatisfaction of some, who end up sad —sad priests—in some sense becoming collectors of antiques or novelties, instead of being shepherds living with "the odor of the sheep." This I ask you: be shepherds, with the "odor of the sheep," make it real, as shepherds among your flock, fishers of men.

—Homily during Chrism Mass on Holy Thursday, March 28, 2013

Those who have demonstrated their aptitude for being innovative and for improving the lives of many people by their ingenuity and professional expertise can further contribute by putting their skills at the service of those who are still living in dire poverty.

—Message to chairman of the World Economic Forum, January 17, 2014

Since we are Christians we also pray to God to touch the hearts of these men and women who enslave because they are also slaves themselves. Slaves of something else: of greed, pride, self-importance, and evil. I pray to you for them but above all I come to you to pray for our humble brothers and sisters . . . who are subjected to this slavery.

—Anniversary of International Convention for the Rights of Migrant Workers, Argentina, July 4, 2008

FAITH & BELIEF

We become fully human when we become more than human, when we let God bring us beyond ourselves in order to attain the fullest truth of our being.

—The Joy of the Gospel

Ours is not a "lab faith," but a "journey faith," a historical faith. God has revealed himself as history, not as a compendium of abstract truths. I am afraid of laboratories because in the laboratory you take the problems and then you bring them home to tame them, to paint them artificially, out of their context. You cannot bring home the frontier, but you have to live on the border and be audacious.

—"A Big Heart Open to God," *America,* September 30, 2013

There is no human experience, no journey of man to God, which cannot be taken up, illumined, and purified by this light.

—"The Light of Faith" letter, June 29, 2013

An authentic faith—which is never comfortable or completely personal— always involves a deep desire to change the world, to transmit values, to leave this earth somehow better that we found it.

—*The Joy of the Gospel*

It's sad to find watered-down Christians, who are just like watered-down wine.

—Angelus prayer in St. Peter's Square, August 31, 2014

•••

I believe in God, not in a Catholic God, there is no Catholic God, there is God and I believe in Jesus Christ, his incarnation.

—*La Repubblica* interview, October 1, 2013

A faith which is lived out in a serious manner gives rise to acts of authentic charity.

—Address to Members of St. Peter's Circle, October 31, 2013

•••

Nor is the light of faith, joined to the truth of love, extraneous to the material world, for love is always lived out in body and spirit; the light of faith is an incarnate light radiating from the luminous life of Jesus.

—"The Light of Faith" letter June 29, 2013

Since many of you do not belong to the Catholic Church and others are non-believers, from the bottom of my heart I give this silent blessing to each and every one of you, respecting the conscience of each one of you but knowing that each one of you is a child of God. May God bless all of you.

—Comments to journalists, March 16, 2013

If a person says that he met God with total certainty and is not touched by a margin of uncertainty, then this is not good. For me, this is an important key. If one has the answers to all the questions—that is the proof that God is not with him. It means that he is a false prophet using religion for himself.

—"A Big Heart Open to God," *America,* September 30, 2013

Yet it is precisely in contemplating Jesus's death that faith grows stronger and receives a dazzling light; then it is revealed as faith in Christ's steadfast love for us, a love capable of embracing death to bring us salvation. This love, which did not recoil before death in order to show its depth, is something I can believe in; Christ's total self-gift overcomes every suspicion and enables me to entrust myself to him completely.

—"The Light of Faith" letter, June 29, 2013

Proselytism is solemn nonsense, it makes no sense. We need to get to know each other, listen to each other and improve our knowledge of the world around us. Sometimes after a meeting I want to arrange another one because new ideas are born and I discover new needs. This is important: to get to know people, listen, expand the circle of ideas. The world is crisscrossed by roads that come closer together and move apart, but the important thing is that they lead towards the Good.

—*La Repubblica* interview, October 1, 2013

There is an urgent need, then, to see once again that faith is a light, for once the flame of faith dies out, all other lights begin to dim.

—"The Light of Faith" letter, June 29, 2013

God is certainly in the past because we can see the footprints. And God is also in the future as a promise. But the "concrete" God, so to speak, is today.

—"A Big Heart Open to God," *America,* September 30, 2013

"Where are your parents?" the judge asked the martyr. He replied: "Our true father is Christ, and our mother is faith in him." For those early Christians, faith, as an encounter with the living God revealed in Christ, was indeed a "mother," for it had brought them to the light and given birth within them to divine life, a new experience and a luminous vision of existence for which they were prepared to bear public witness to the end.

—"The Light of Faith" letter, June 29, 2013

It is from contemplation, from a strong friendship with the Lord that the capacity is born in us to live and to bring the love of God, his mercy, his tenderness, to others. And also our work with brothers in need, our charitable works of mercy, lead us to the Lord, because it is in the needy brother and sister that we see the Lord himself.

—Angelus, July 21, 2013

Whenever we encounter another person in love, we learn something new about God. Whenever our eyes are opened to acknowledge the other, we grow in the light of faith and knowledge of God. If we want to advance in the spiritual life, then, we must constantly be missionaries.

—*The Joy of the Gospel*

•••

From my point of view, God is the light that illuminates the darkness, even if it does not dissolve it, and a spark of divine light is within each of us.

—*La Repubblica* interview, October 1, 2013

Faith, on the other hand, by revealing the love of God the Creator, enables us to respect nature all the more, and to discern in it a grammar written by the hand of God and a dwelling place entrusted to our protection and care.

—"The Light of Faith" letter, June 29, 2013

The Holy Spirit makes us look to the horizon and drive us to the very outskirts of existence in order to proclaim life in Jesus Christ. Let us ask ourselves: do we tend to stay closed in on ourselves, on our group, or do we let the Holy Spirit open us to mission?

—Homily, May 19, 2013

This is [God's] invitation, juxtaposed against so many injuries that wound us and can tempt us temptation to be hardened: Rend your hearts to experience, in serene and silent prayer, the gentle tenderness of God.

—Lenten Letter of 2013, March 24, 2013

Dear friends, it is certainly necessary to give bread to the hungry—this is an act of justice. But there is also a deeper hunger, the hunger for a happiness that only God can satisfy, the hunger for dignity.

—To the Community of Varginha in Rio de Janeiro, July 25, 2013

•••

If following Him seems difficult, don't be afraid, trust Him, be confident that He is close to you, He is with you, and He will give you the peace you are looking for and the strength to live as He would have you do.

—Easter Vigil Homily, March 31, 2013

When Jesus asked Peter, "Do you love Me?" his "Yes" was not the result of an effort of will, it was not the fruit of a "decision" made by the young man Simon: it was the emergence, the coming to the surface of an entire vein of tenderness and adherence that made sense because of the esteem he had for Him—therefore an act of reason, which is why he couldn't not say "Yes."

—Speech at the International Book Fair in Buenos Aires, April 27, 2001

You can prove that God exists, but you will never be able, using the force of persuasion, to make anyone encounter God. This is pure grace.

—Speech at the International Book Fair in Buenos, April 27, 2001

•••

Jesus is Love incarnate. He is not simply a teacher of wisdom, he is not an ideal for which we strive while knowing that we are hopelessly distant from it. He is the meaning of life and history, who has pitched his tent in our midst.

—Midnight Mass on Christmas Eve, December 24, 2013

It is impossible to believe on our own. Faith is not simply an individual decision which takes place in the depths of the believer's heart, nor a completely private relationship between the "I" of the believer and the divine "Thou," between an autonomous subject and God. By its very nature, faith is open to the "We" of the Church; it always takes place within her communion.

—"The Light of Faith" letter, June 29, 2013

Jesus does not force you to be a Christian. But if you say you are a Christian you must believe that Jesus has all the strength—the only one who has the strength—to renew the world, to renew your life, to renew your family, to renew the community, to renew everybody.

—Homily during Mass of the Sacrament of Confirmation, February 18, 2012

•••

Faith involves deciding to be with the Lord so as to live with him and to share him with our brethren.

—Letter on the Year of Faith, October 1, 2012

THE CHURCH

I dream of a Church that is a mother and shepherdess. The Church's ministers must be merciful, take responsibility for the people, and accompany them like the good Samaritan, who washes, cleans, and raises up his neighbor.

—Vatican Insider, *September 19, 2013*

"A good Catholic doesn't meddle in politics." That's not true. That is not a good path. A good Catholic meddles in politics, offering the best of himself, so that those who govern can govern. But what is the best that we can offer to those who govern? Prayer!

—*Vatican Radio,* September 16, 2013

We must restore hope to young people, help the old, be open to the future, spread love. Be poor among the poor. We need to include the excluded and preach peace.

—*La Repubblica* interview, October 1, 2013

•••

The Church which "goes forth" is a community of missionary disciples who take the first step, who are involved and supportive, who bear fruit and rejoice.

—*The Joy of the Gospel*

I prefer a Church which is bruised, hurting and dirty because it has been out on the streets, rather than a Church which is unhealthy from being confined and from clinging to its own security.

—*The Joy of the Gospel*

We have to avoid the spiritual sickness of a self-referential church. It's true that when you get out into the street, as happens to every man and woman, there can be accidents. However, if the Church remains closed in on itself, self-referential, it gets old.

—*National Catholic Reporter*, March 3, 2013

Jesus teaches us another way: Go out. Go out and share your testimony, go out and interact with your brothers, go out and share, go out and ask. Become the Word in body as well as spirit.

—Quoted by NBC News, March 13, 2013

In a Christian community, division is one of the gravest sins, because it marks it not as the work of God but of the Devil."

—Weekly address at St. Peter's Square, August 27, 2014

•••

Women are the most beautiful thing God has made. The Church is a woman.

—*Il Messaggero* interview, July 1, 2014

Instead of being just a church that welcomes and receives by keeping the doors open, let us try also to be a church that finds new roads, that is able to step outside itself and go to those who do not attend Mass, to those who have quit or are indifferent.

—"A Big Heart Open to God," *America*, September 30, 2013

I must look at [the Catholic Church's] sins and shortcomings as I would look at my mother's sins and shortcomings. And when I think of her, I remember the good and beautiful things she has achieved, more than her weaknesses and defects.

—*Vatican Insider* interview, February 24, 2012

I see the Church as a field hospital after battle. It is useless to ask a seriously injured person if he has high cholesterol and about the level of his blood sugars! You have to heal his wounds. Then we can talk about everything else. Heal the wounds, heal the wounds. . . . And you have to start from the ground up.

—"A Big Heart Open to God," *America,* September 30, 2013

I would like a more missionary Church, one that is not so staid.

—Meeting with seminarians and novices, July 6, 2013

•••

The Church is or should go back to being a community of God's people, and priests, pastors and bishops who have the care of souls, are at the service of the people of God.

—*La Repubblica* interview, October 1, 2013

Vanity, showing off, is an attitude that reduces spirituality to a worldly thing, which is the worst sin that could be committed in the Church.

—*Vatican Insider* interview, February 24, 2012

The woman is essential for the Church. Mary, a woman, is more important than the bishops. I say this because we must not confuse the function with the dignity. We must therefore investigate further the role of women in the Church. We have to work harder to develop a profound theology of the woman. Only by making this step will it be possible to better reflect on their function within the Church.

—"A Big Heart Open to God," *America*, September 30, 2013

The Church is a mother: she has to go
out to heal those who are hurting, with
mercy. If the Lord never tires of forgiving,
we have no other choice than this: first of
all, to care for those who are hurting.

—Press conference on return flight from
World Youth Day in Rio de Janeiro,
July 28, 2013

In a culture paradoxically suffering
from anonymity and at the same time
obsessed with the details of other people's
lives, shamelessly given over to morbid
curiosity, the Church must look more
closely and sympathetically at others
whenever necessary.

—*The Joy of the Gospel*

It is Mass itself which integrates us into
Christ's immense work of salvation, which
hones our spiritual vision so that we can
perceive his love: his "prophecy in action."

—Message to the National Eucharistic
Congress of Germany in Cologne,
June 5–9, 2013

When I think of the parish priests who knew the names of their parishioners, who went to visit them; even as one of them told me: "I know the name of each family's dog." They even knew the dog's name! How nice it was! What could be more beautiful than this?

—Address at Cathedral of San Rufino, Assisi, October 4, 2013

The thing the Church needs most today is the ability to heal wounds and to warm the hearts of the faithful.

—"A Big Heart Open to God," *America*, September 30, 2013

The Church is not distinct from us, but should be seen as the totality of believers, as the "we" of Christians: I, you, we all are part of the Church. . . . The Church is all of us: from the baby just baptized to the Bishop, the Pope; we are all the Church and we are all equal in the eyes of God!

—Address to General Audience, September 11, 2013

There is not one Church for Europeans, one for Africans, one for Americans, one for Asians, one for those who live in Oceania. No, she is one and the same everywhere. It is like being in a family: some of its members may be far away, scattered across the world, but the deep bonds that unite all the members of a family stay solid however great the distance.

—*The Church of Mercy,* April 2014

What is God's plan? It is to make of us all a single family of his children, in which each person feels that God is close and feels loved by him, as in the Gospel parable, feels the warmth of being God's family.

—Address to general audience in Saint Peter's Square, May 29, 2013

In our ecclesiastical region there are priests who don't baptize the children of single mothers because they weren't conceived in the sanctity of marriage. These are today's hypocrites. Those who clericalize the Church. Those who separate the people of God from salvation.

—Quoted in the *Guardian*, March 2013

If the Church, in her complete and real dimension, loses women, she risks becoming sterile.

—Homily at Cathedral of San Sebastian in Rio de Janeiro, July 27, 2013

The Church is called to come out of herself and to go to the peripheries, not only in the geographical sense but also to go to the existential peripheries: those of the mystery of sin, of pain, of injustice, of ignorance, and of religious indifference, of thought, of all misery.

—Speech in Havana, Cuba, March 2013

The first fruit of baptism is that you belong to the Church, to the people of God. One cannot understand a Christian without the Church.

—Homily at Santa Marta, January 30, 2014

•••

Do we pray for the Church? Each day at the Mass, but at home, no? When do we pray? We need to pray to the Lord for the whole Church, all over the world.

—Homily at Santa Marta, January 30, 2014

YOUTH

Young people are the window through which the future enters the world.

—Welcome address at the 28th World Youth Day, July 22, 2013

The most serious of the evils that afflict the world these days are youth unemployment and the loneliness of the old. The old need care and companionship; the young need work and hope but have neither one nor the other, and the problem is they don't even look for them anymore. They have been crushed by the present.

—*La Repubblica* interview, October 1, 2013

Our generation will show that it can rise to the promise found in each young person when we know how to give them space. This means that we have to create the material and spiritual conditions for their full development . . . and to awaken in them their greatest potential as builders of their own destiny, sharing responsibility for the future of everyone.

—Welcome ceremony in the Garden of Guanabara Palace, Rio de Janeiro, July 22, 2013

Crisis is not a bad thing. It is true that the crisis causes us suffering but we—and first and foremost all you young people— must know how to interpret the crisis. What does this crisis mean? What must I do to help us to come through this crisis?

—To the students of the Jesuit Schools of Italy and Albania, June 7, 2013

Dear young people, please, don't be observers of life, but get involved. Jesus did not remain an observer, but he immersed himself. Don't be observers, but immerse yourself in the reality of life, as Jesus did.

—Prayer Vigil on World Youth Day, July 27, 2013

These young people are from every continent, they speak many languages, they bring with them different cultures, and yet they also find in Christ the answer to their highest aspirations, held in common, and they can satisfy the hunger for a pure truth and an authentic love which binds them together in spite of differences.

—Welcome address at the 28th World Youth Day, July 22, 2013

Christ has confidence in young people and entrusts them with the very future of his mission, "Go and make disciples." Go beyond the confines of what is humanly possible and create a world of brothers and sisters!

—Welcome Ceremony in the Garden of Guanabara Palace, Rio de Janeiro, July 22, 2013

•••

Dear young people, Christ asks you to be wide awake and alert, to see the things in life that really matter.

—Twitter @Pontifex, August 15, 2014

Young people are a powerful engine for the Church and for society. They do not need material things alone; also and above all, they need to have held up to them those non-material values which are the spiritual heart of a people, the memory of a people.

—Homily on World Youth Day, July 27, 2013

And then I would like to speak especially to you young people: be committed to your daily duties, your study, your work, to relationships of friendship, to helping towards others; your future also depends on how you live these precious years of your life.

—Feast of St. Joseph Speech, May 1, 2013

Dear young people, I saw you in the procession as you were coming in; I think of you celebrating around Jesus, waving your olive branches. I think of you crying out his name and expressing your joy at being with him! You have an important part in the celebration of faith! You bring us the joy of faith and you tell us that we must live the faith with a young heart, always: a young heart, even at the age of seventy or eighty.

—Palm Sunday Homily, March 24, 2013

Dear young people, do not be mediocre; the Christian life challenges us with great ideals.

—Twitter @Pontifex, July 15, 2014

•••

Children and the elderly are the two poles of life and the most vulnerable as well, often the most forgotten.

—Address to the Council for Family, August 10, 2014

Jesus did not say: "One of you go," but "All of you go": we are sent together. Dear young friends, be aware of the companionship of the whole Church and also the communion of the saints on this mission. . . . Jesus did not call the Apostles to live in isolation, he called them to form a group, a community.

—Homily on World Youth Day, July 27, 2013

Do not be afraid of commitment, of sacrifice and do not look with fear towards the future; keep your hope alive: there is always a light on the horizon.

—Feast of St. Joseph Speech, May 1, 2013

•••

Dear young people, listen within: Christ is knocking at the door of your heart.

—Twitter @Pontifex, September 20, 2014

Our life is made up of time, and time is a gift from God, so it is important that it be used in good and fruitful actions.

—Meeting with German altar servers in St. Peter's Square as quoted by Reuters, August 6, 2014

As young Christians, whether you are workers or students, whether you have already begun a career or have answered the call to marriage, religious life, or the priesthood, you are not only a part of the *future* of the Church; you are also a necessary and beloved part of the Church's *present*!

—Homily at Closing Mass of Sixth Annual Asian Youth Day, August 17, 2014

No one who sleeps can sing, dance, or rejoice. I don't like to see young people who are sleeping. No! Wake up! Go!

—Homily at Closing Mass of Sixth Annual Asian Youth Day, August 17, 2014

•••

I think we have to work harder for the common good of children.

—*Il Messaggero* interview, July 1, 2014

I ask the Lord Jesus to enable many young people to discover that burning zeal which joy kindles in our hearts as soon as we have the stroke of boldness needed to respond willingly to his call.

—Homily during Holy Chrism Mass, April 17, 2014

Let Christ turn your natural optimism into Christian hope, your energy into moral virtue, your good will into genuine self-sacrificing love! This is the path you are called to take.

—Homily at Closing Mass of Sixth Annual Asian Youth Day, August 17, 2014

Yes, our heart is built on the memory of those men and women who have brought us closer to sources of life and hope that can also be drawn upon by those who follow us. It is the memory of the inheritance we have received and that we must, in turn, transmit to our children.

—Memorial for the priest Giacomo Tantardini in Buenos Aires, May 6, 2012

Chatting on the Internet or with smartphones, watching TV soap operas, and the products of technological progress should simplify and improve the quality of life, but distract attention away from what is really important.

—Meeting with German altar servers in St. Peter's Square (quoted by Reuters), August 6, 2014

Crossing the threshold of faith means not being ashamed to have the heart of a child who, because he still believes in impossible things, can live in hope—the one thing that is capable of giving meaning and transforming history.

—Letter on the Year of Faith, October 1, 2012

LIFE

✝

Dear brothers and sisters, the Church loves you! Be an active presence in the community, as living cells, as living stones.

—Homily on the Day of Confraternities and Popular Piety, May 5, 2013

Together with a culture of work, there must be a culture of leisure as gratification. To put it another way: people who work must take the time to relax, to be with their families, to enjoy themselves, read, listen to music, play a sport.

—*Pope Francis: His Life in His Own Words*

When one lives attached to money, pride, or power, it is impossible to be truly happy.

—Twitter @Pontifex, July 24, 2014

•••

Our life is made up of time, and time is a gift from God, so it is important that it be used in good and fruitful actions.

—Address to German Altar Servers, August 5, 2014

What we are called to respect in each person is first of all his life, his physical integrity, his dignity and the rights deriving from that dignity, his reputation, his property, his ethnic and cultural identity, his ideas and his political choices. We are therefore called to think, speak, and write respectfully of the other, not only in his presence, but always and everywhere, avoiding unfair criticism or defamation . . . all forms of media have a role to play in achieving this goal.

—Message to Muslims around the world, July 10, 2013

One of the more serious temptations which stifles boldness and zeal is a defeatism which turns us into querulous and disillusioned pessimists, sourpusses. Nobody can go off to battle unless he is fully convinced of victory beforehand. If we start without confidence, we have already lost half the battle and we bury our talents.

— *The Joy of the Gospel*

This will benefit you throughout life. Let us say it together: a clean defeat is always better than a dirty victory.

—Address to students and teachers from across Italy, May 10, 2014

A people that doesn't take care of its grandparents and treat them well is a people with no future.

—St. Peter's Square, September 29, 2014

•••

In my life I have learned, and I still do, that mistakes are the best teachers.

—From interview with Belgian youth, March 31, 2014

No vocation is born of itself or lives for itself. A vocation flows from the heart of God and blossoms in the good soil of faithful people, in the experience of fraternal love. Did not Jesus say: "By this all men will know that you are my disciples, if you have love for one another"?

—Message for the 51st World Day of Prayer for Vocations, May 11, 2014

Let what you teach be nourishment for the people of God. Let the holiness of your lives be a delightful fragrance to Christ's faithful, so that by word and example you may build up the house which is God's Church.

—Homily, April 21, 2013

Gifts [are] given not to be hidden, but to be shared with others. They are not given for the benefit of the one who receives them, but for the use of the People of God.

—Address to General Audience, November 6, 2013

•••

Let us not leave in our wake a swath of destruction and death which will affect our own lives and those of future generations.

—*The Joy of the Gospel*

In the Gospel, Jesus continuously repeats: Be not afraid, be not afraid. Why does He repeat that so often? Because He knows that fear is "normal." . . . You should learn to delineate your fear, because there is good and bad fear. Good fear is like prudence, a careful attitude. Bad fear is fear that limits you. It makes you small. It paralyses you, prevents you from doing things. You must lose that fear.

—From interview with Belgian youth, March 31, 2014

Continue to overcome apathy, offering a Christian response to the social and political anxieties which are arising in various parts of the world. I ask you to be builders of the world, to work for a better world.

—Prayer Vigil on World Youth Day, July 27, 2013

Work must be combined with the preservation of creation so that this may be responsibly safeguarded for future generations. Creation is not a good to be exploited but a gift to look after.

—Meeting with workers in Cagliari, September 22, 2013

Be active members! Go on the offensive! Play down the field, build a better world, a world of brothers and sisters, a world of justice, of love, of peace, of fraternity, of solidarity.

—Quoted by MercatorNet, from Prayer Vigil on World Youth Day, July 30, 2013

In the heart of every man and woman is the desire for a full life, including that irrepressible longing for fraternity which draws us to fellowship with others and enables us to see them not as enemies or rivals, but as brothers and sisters to be accepted and embraced.

—Message for World Day of Peace,
January 1, 2014

I can say that the most beautiful and natural expressions of joy which I have seen in my life were in poor people who had little to hold on to.

—*The Joy of the Gospel*

Fraternal relations between people, and cooperation in building a more just society—these are not an idealistic dream, but the fruit of a concerted effort on the part of all, in service of the common good. I encourage you in this commitment to the common good, a commitment which demands of everyone wisdom, prudence, and generosity.

—Meeting with Brazil's Leaders of Society during World Youth Day, July 27, 2013

Our daily problems and worries can wrap us up in ourselves, in sadness and bitterness . . . and that is where death is. That is not the place to look for the One who is alive! Let the risen Jesus enter your life, welcome him as a friend, with trust: he is life!

—Easter Vigil Homily, March 31, 2013

And here the first word that I wish to say to you: joy! Do not be men and women of sadness: a Christian can never be sad! Never give way to discouragement!

—Palm Sunday Homily, March 24, 2013

•••

Work is part of God's loving plan, we are called to cultivate and care for all the goods of creation and in this way participate in the work of creation!

—Feast of St. Joseph Speech, May 1, 2013

How often does Love have to tell us: Why do you look for the living among the dead?

—Easter Vigil Homily, March 31, 2013

•••

An evangelizer must never look like someone who has just come back from a funeral.

—*The Joy of the Gospel*

The perfect family doesn't exist, nor is there a perfect husband or a perfect wife, and let's not talk about the perfect mother-in-law! It's just us sinners. . . . A healthy family life requires frequent use of three phrases: "May I?" "Thank you," and "I'm sorry."

—Meeting with engaged couples, February 14, 2014

He who has hope lives in a different manner; he has been given a new life.

—Catechesis at the 49th International Eucharistic Congress in Quebec, June 22, 2008

•••

The path is not always a smooth one, free of disagreements, otherwise it would not be human. It is a demanding journey, at times difficult, and at times turbulent, but such is life!

—From the Holy Mass with the Rite of Marriage, September 14, 2014

Let us ask ourselves today: Are we open to "God's surprises"? Or are we closed and fearful before the newness of the Holy Spirit? Do we have the courage to strike out along the new paths which God's newness sets before us, or do we resist, barricaded in transient structures which have lost their capacity for openness to what is new?

—Homily during Solemnity of the Pentecost, May 19, 2013